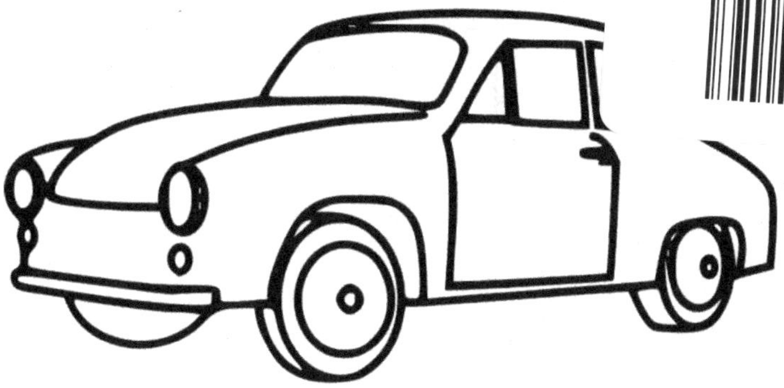

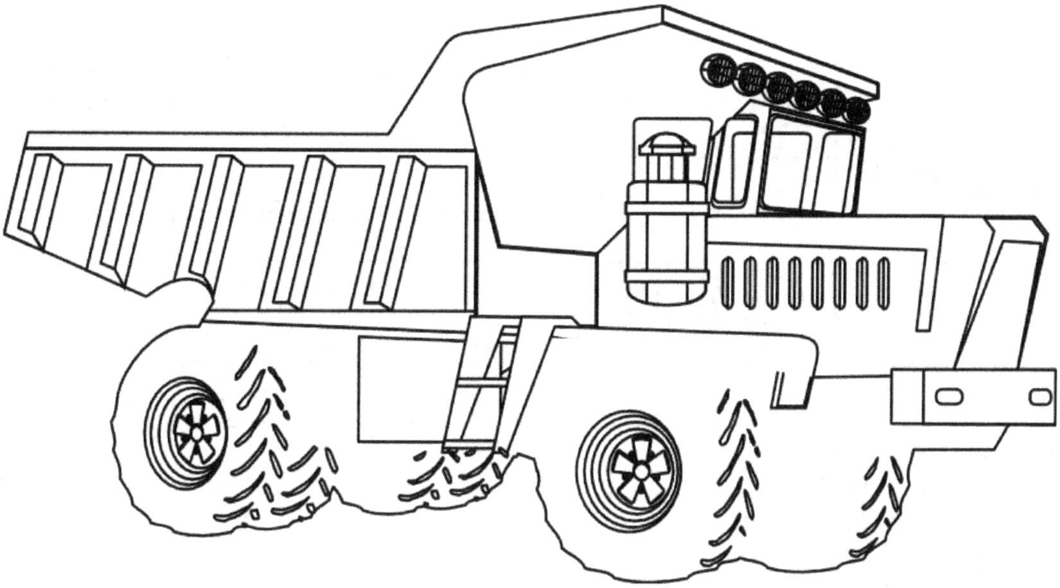

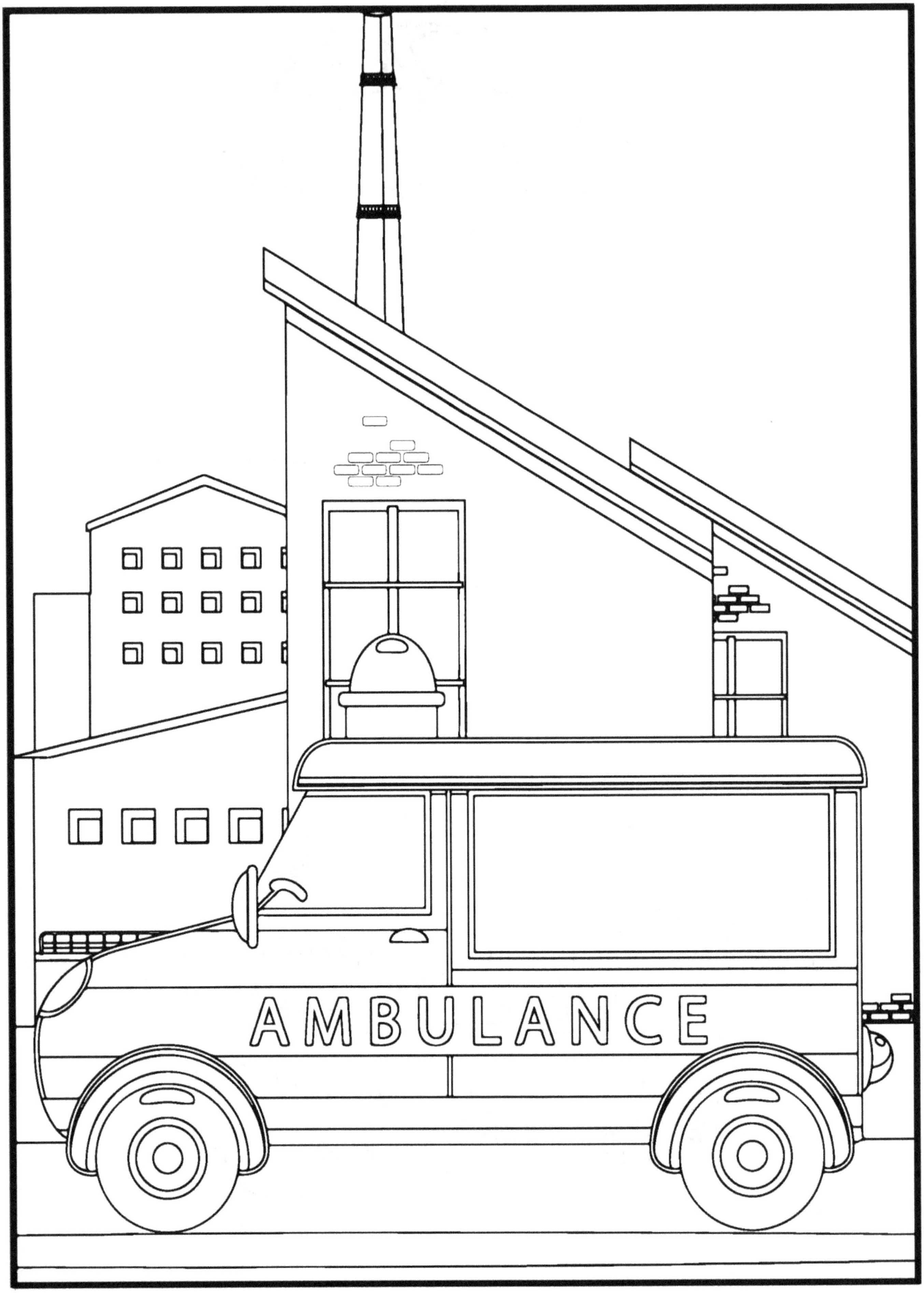
AMBULANCE

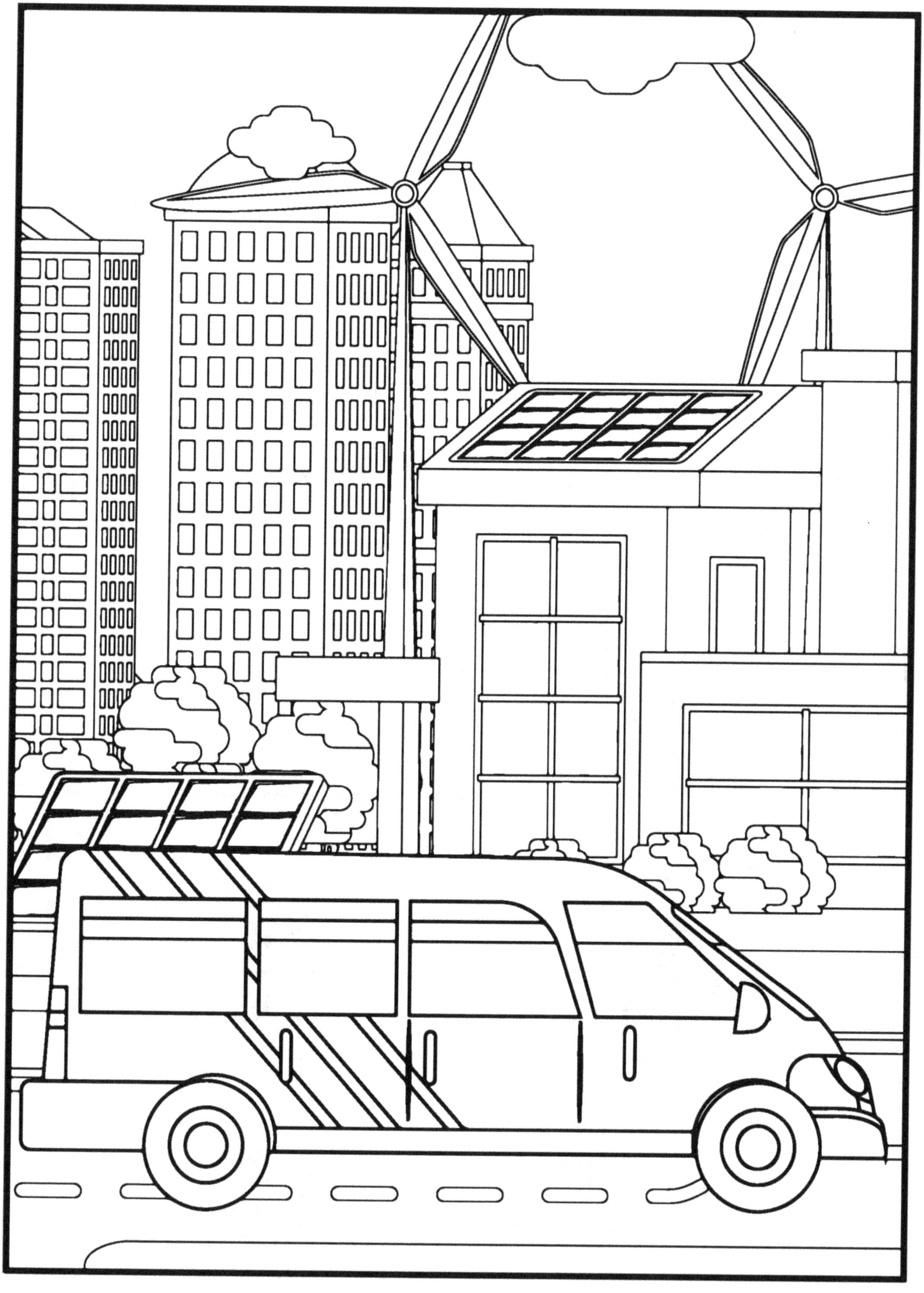

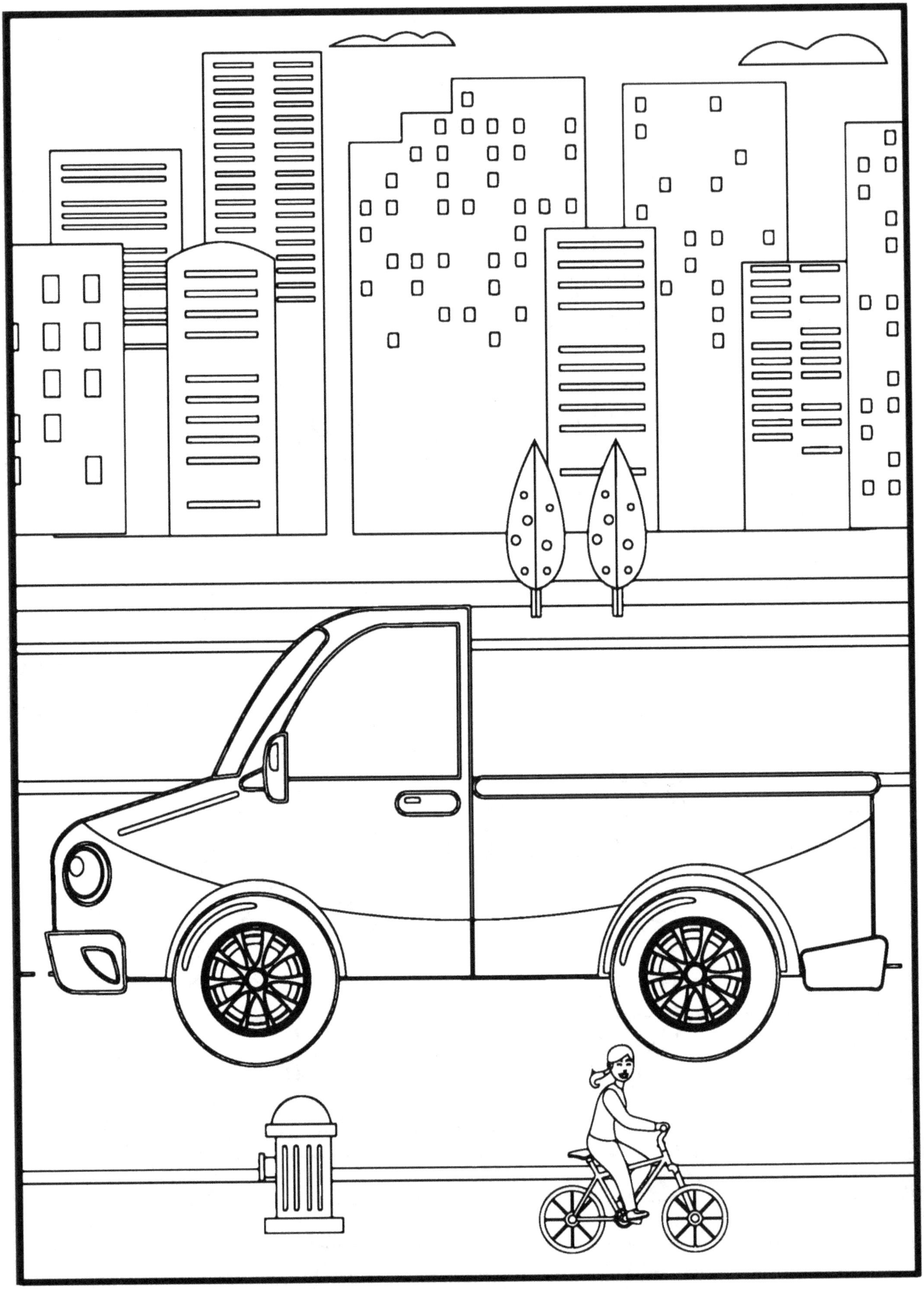

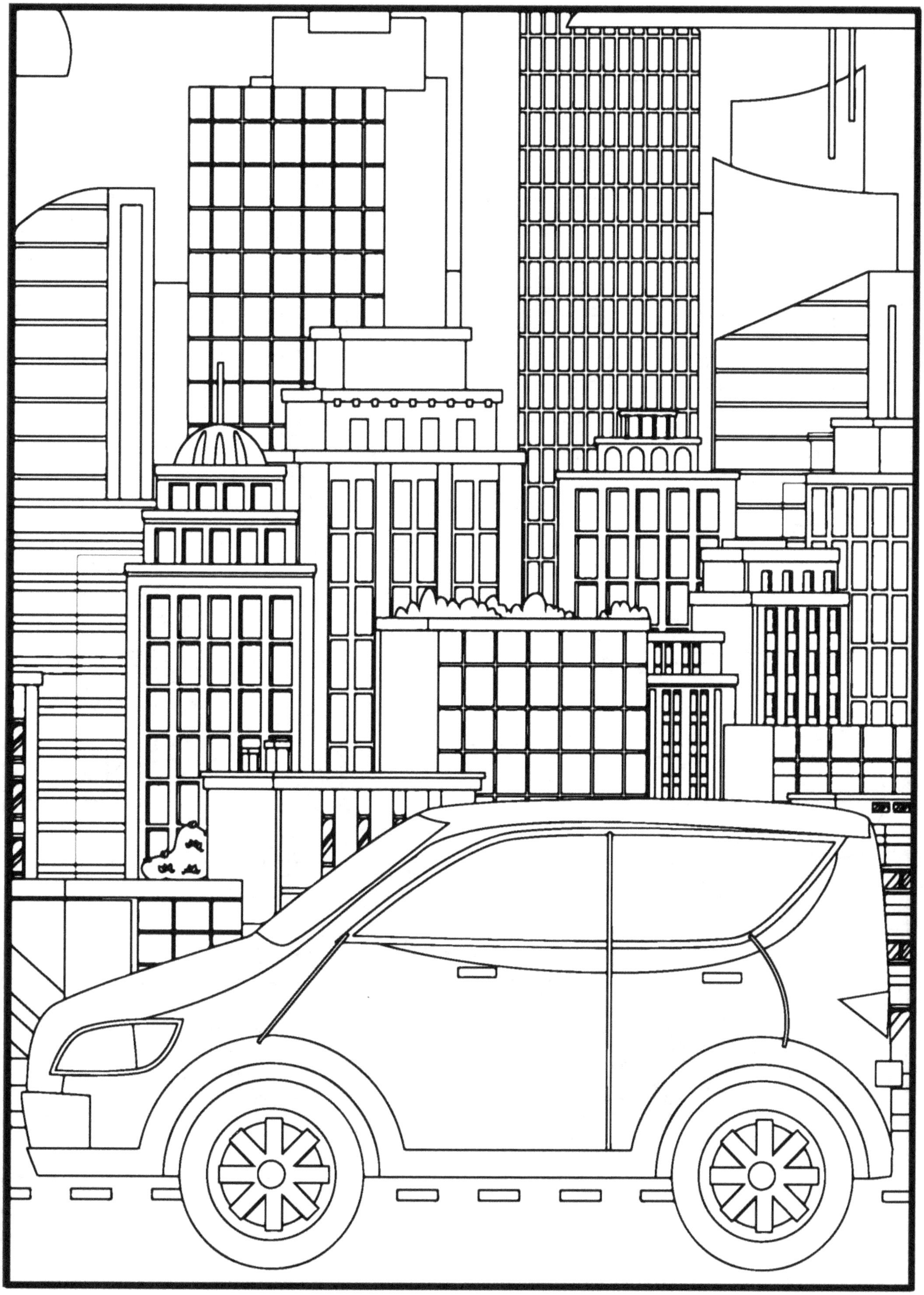

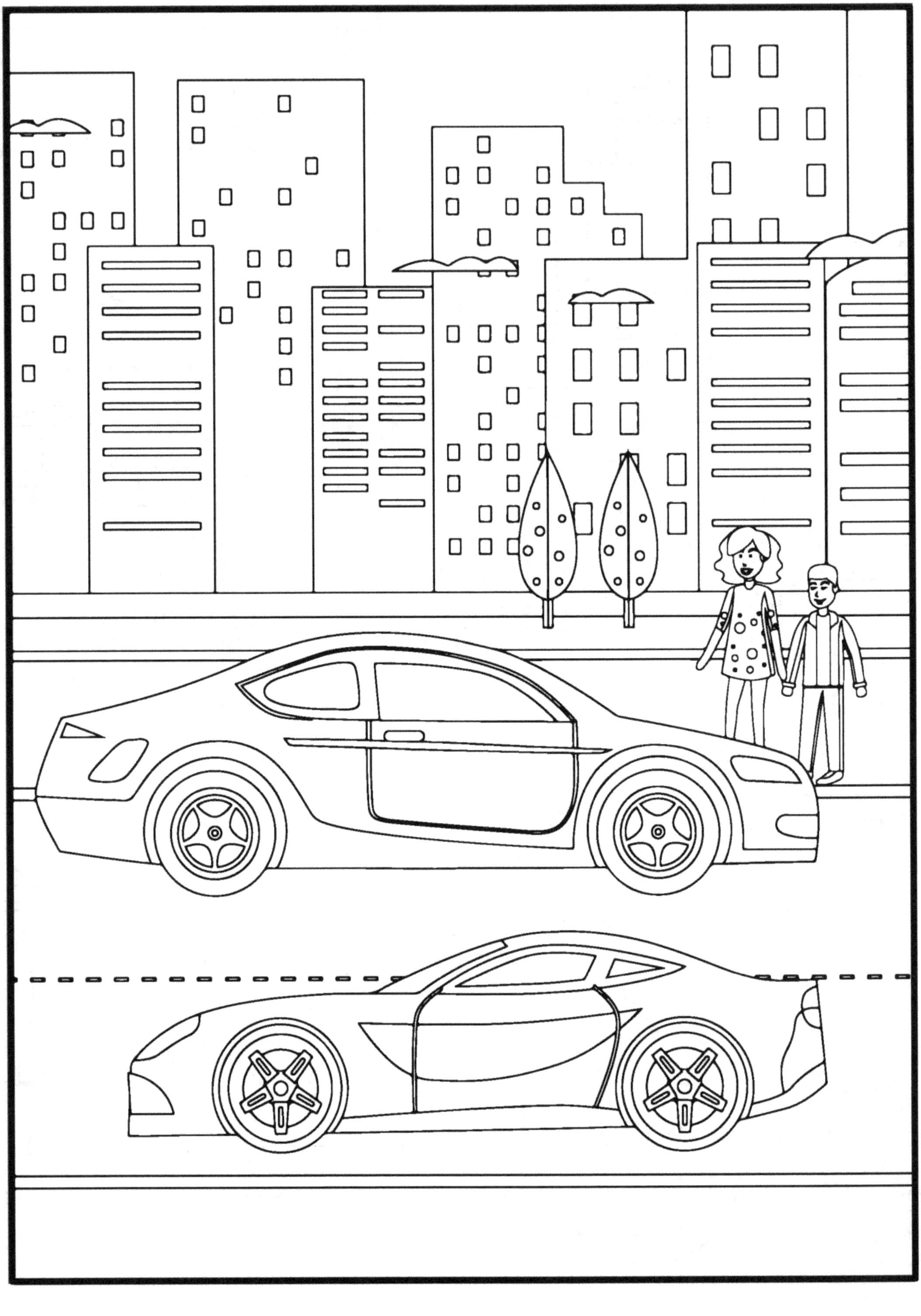

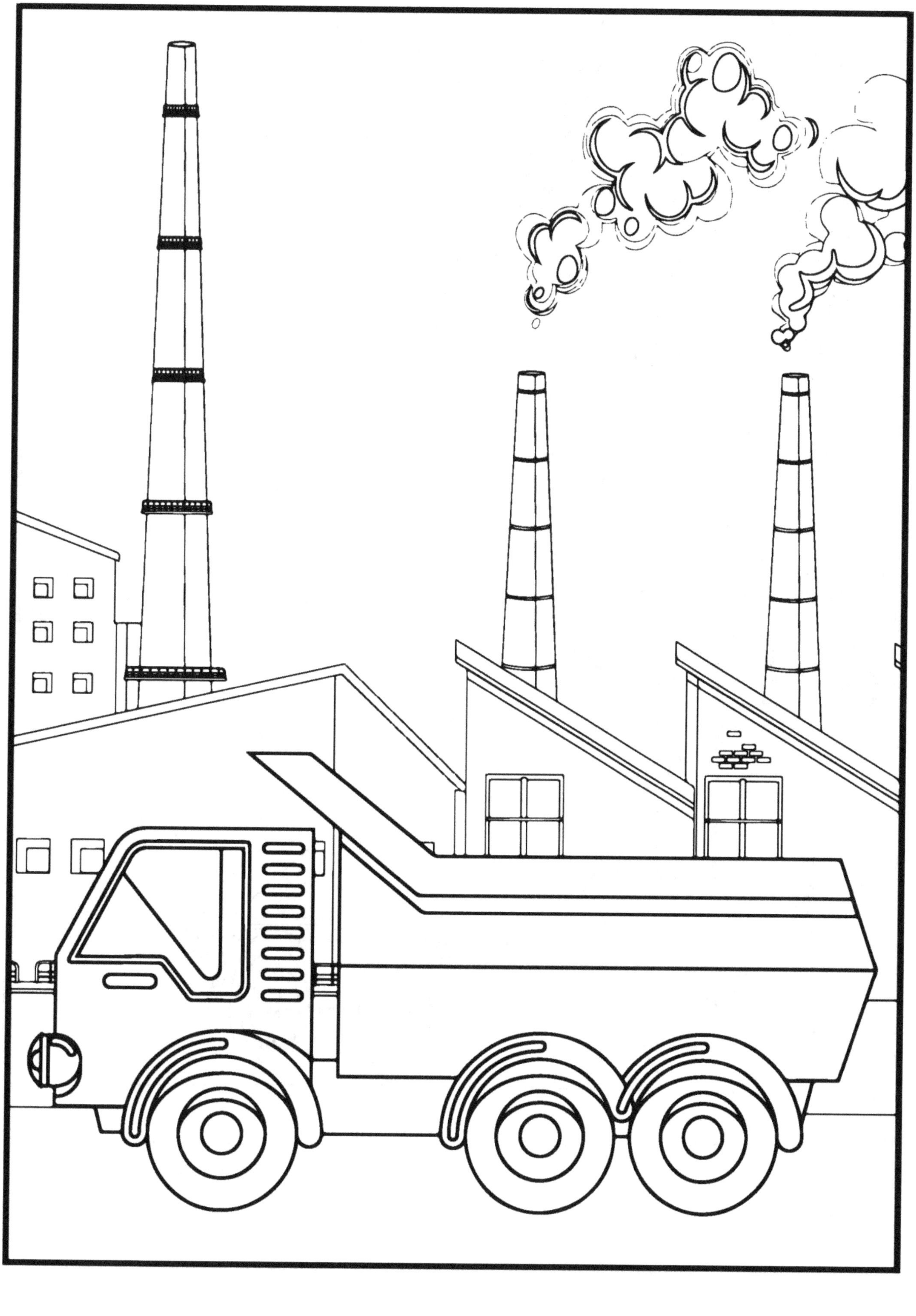

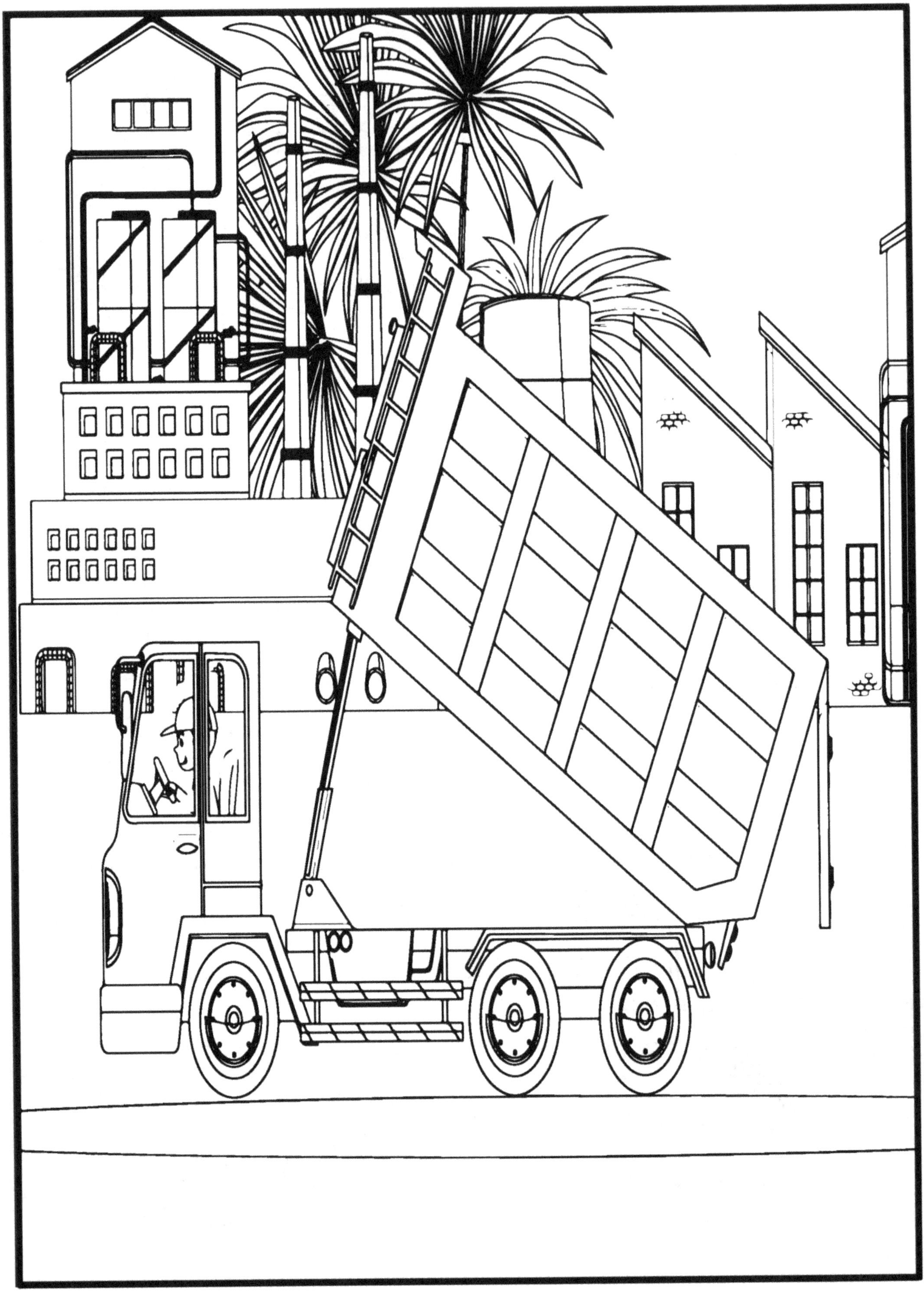

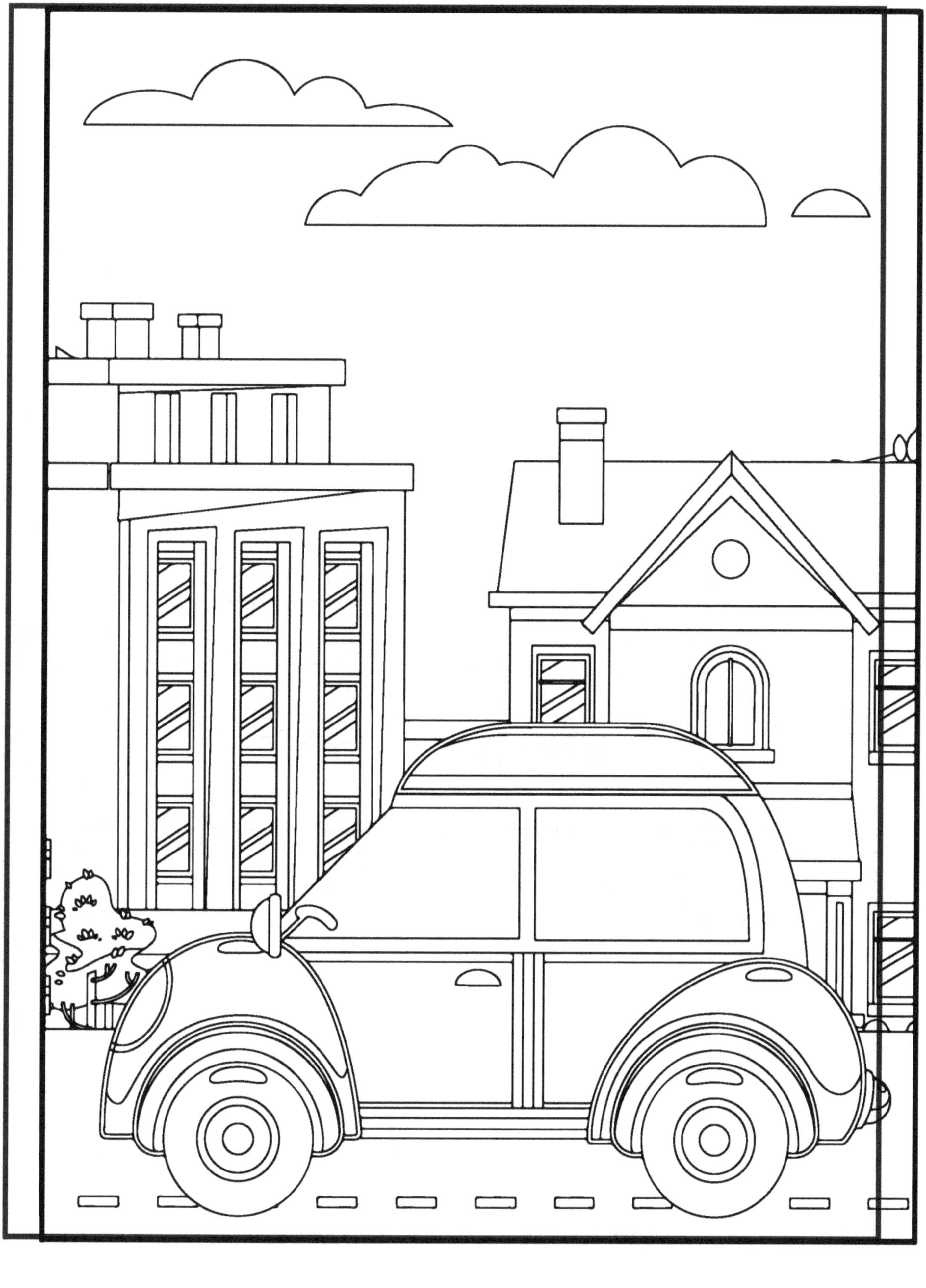

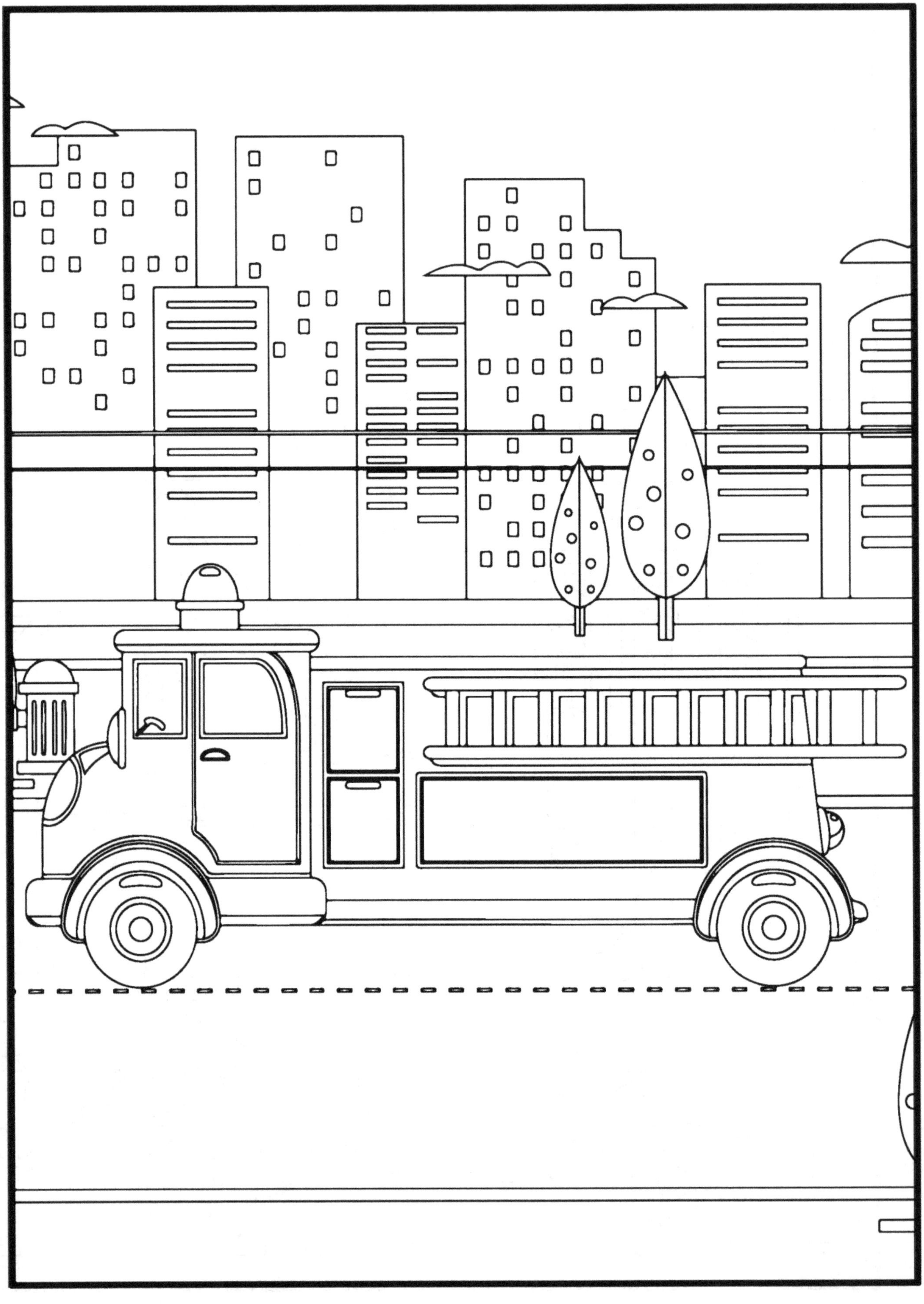

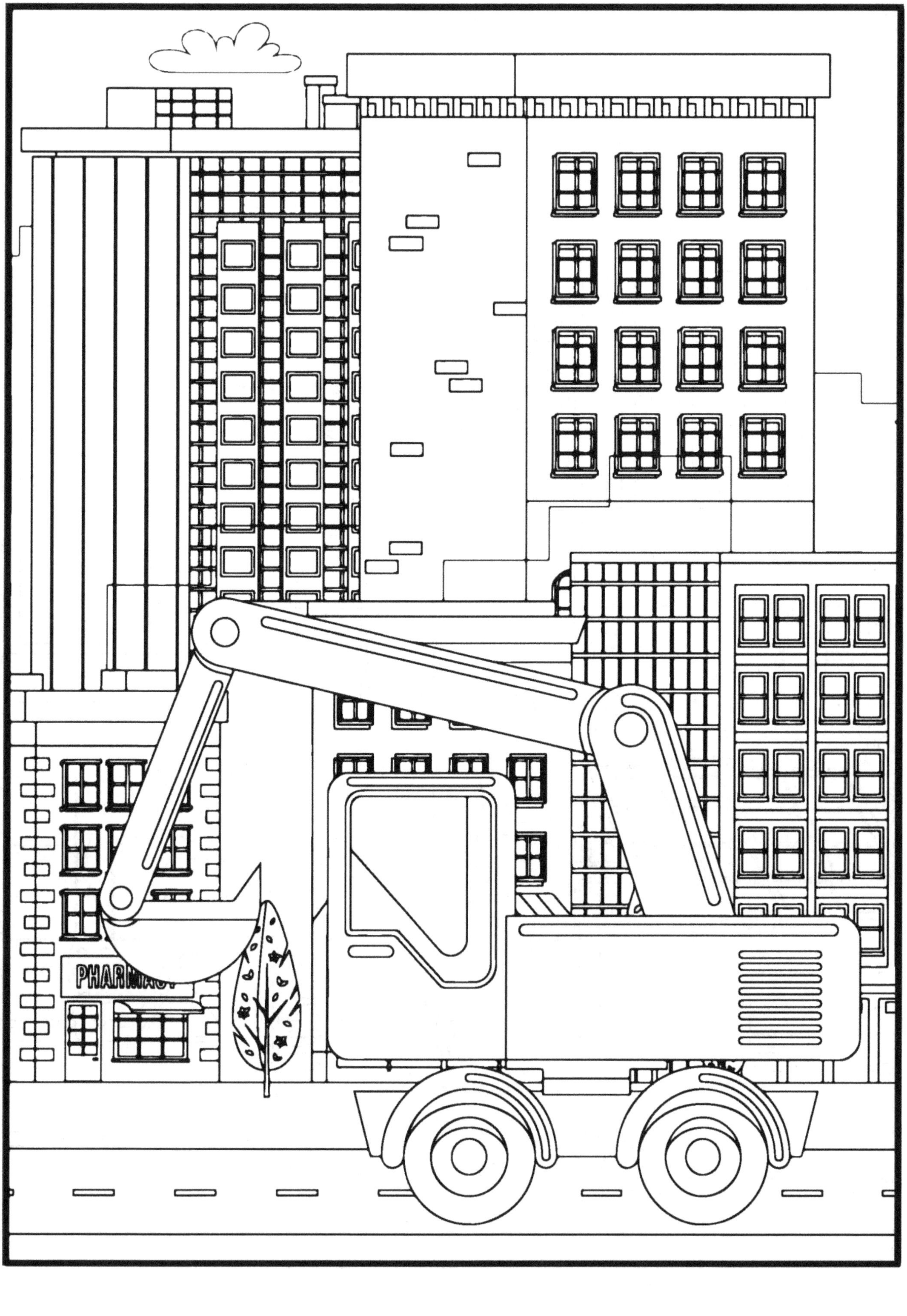
PHARMACY

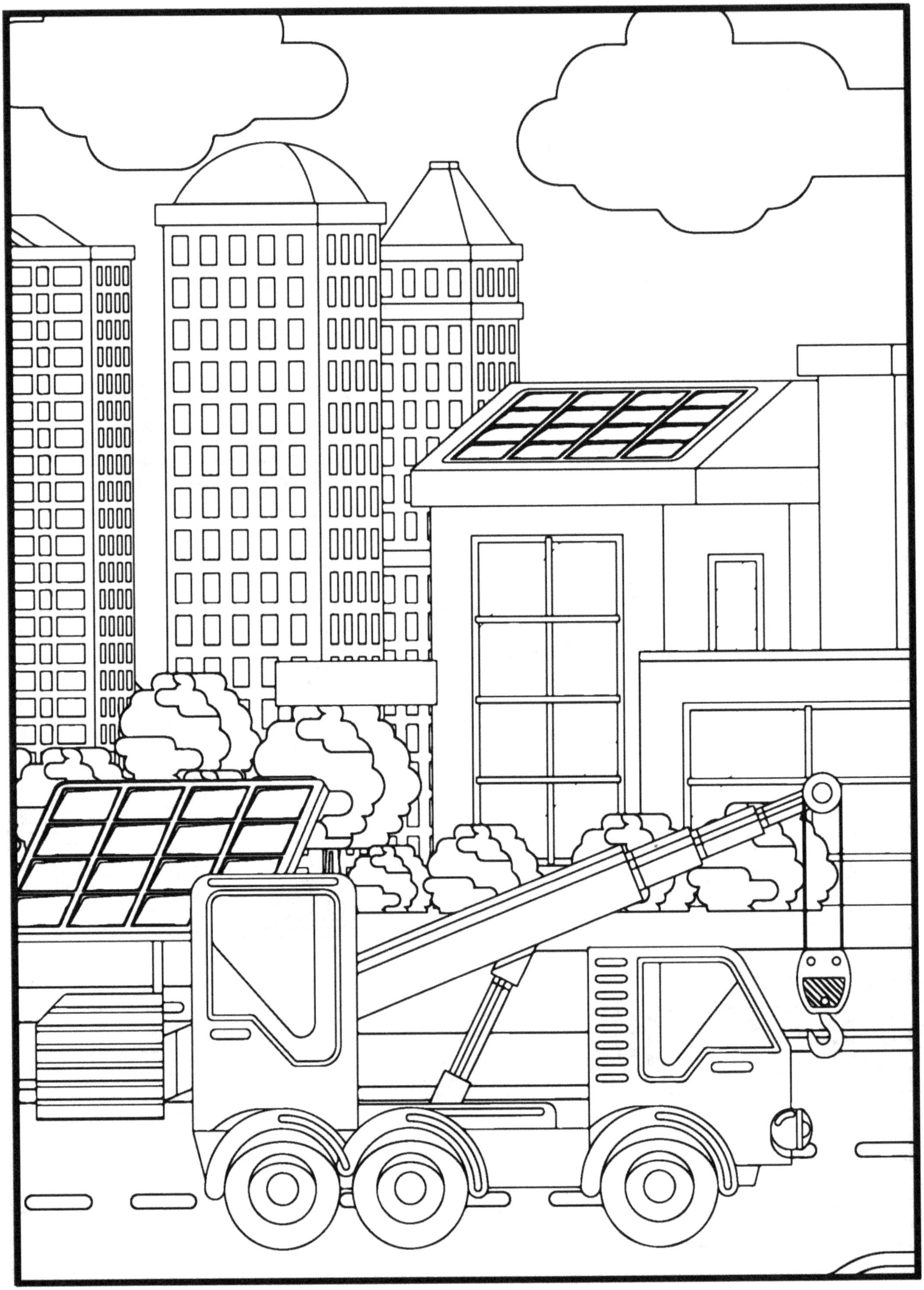

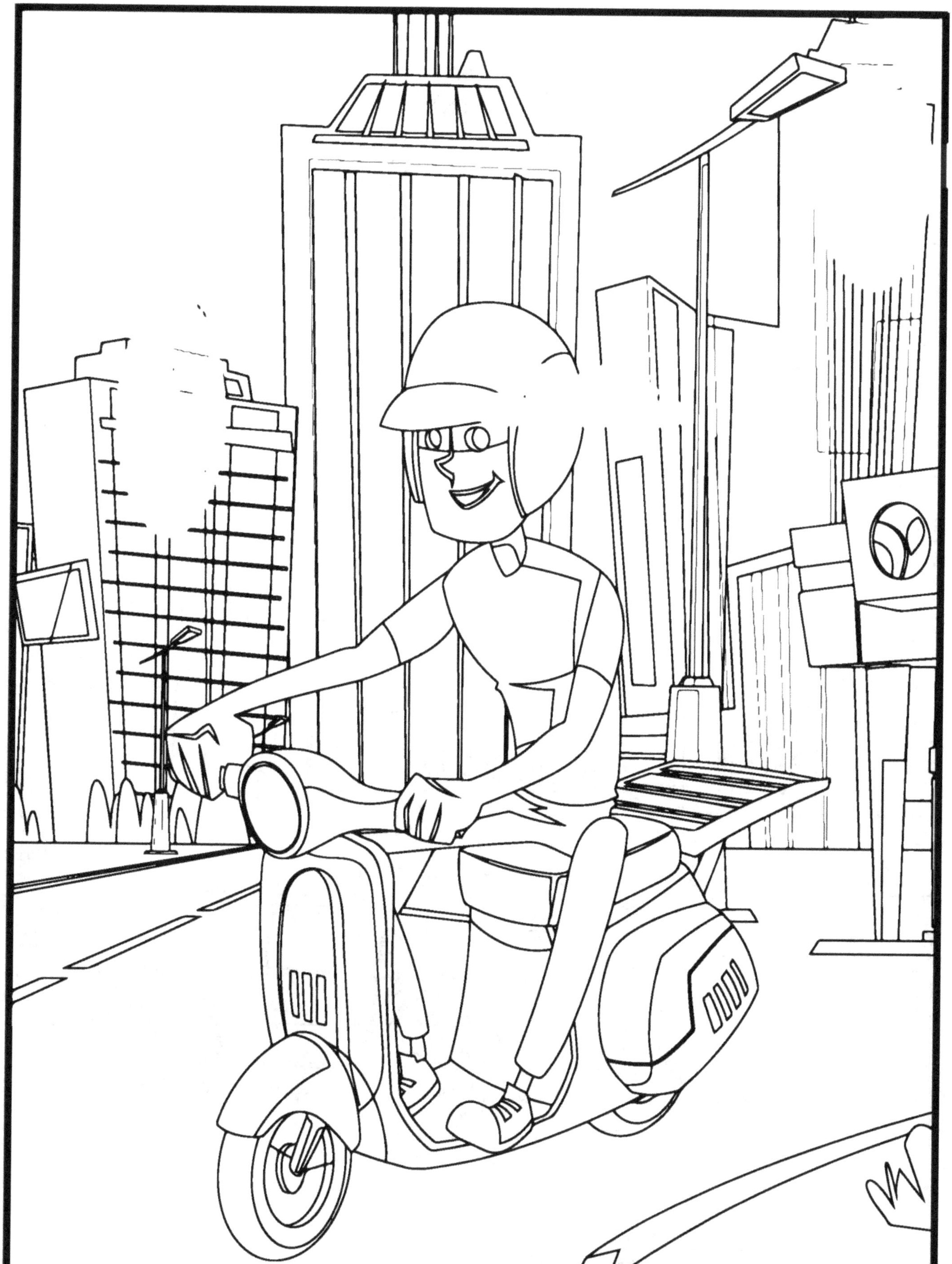

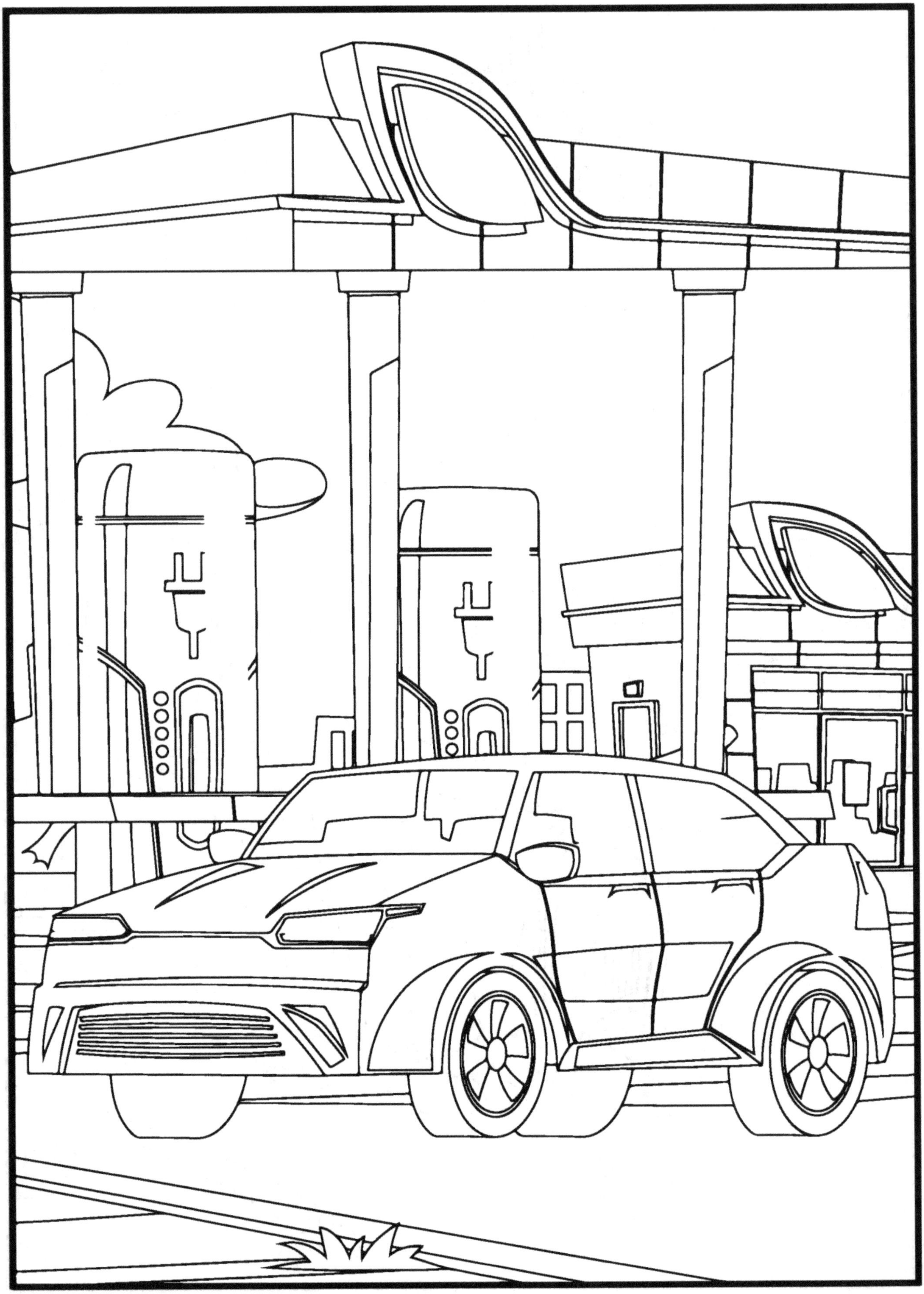

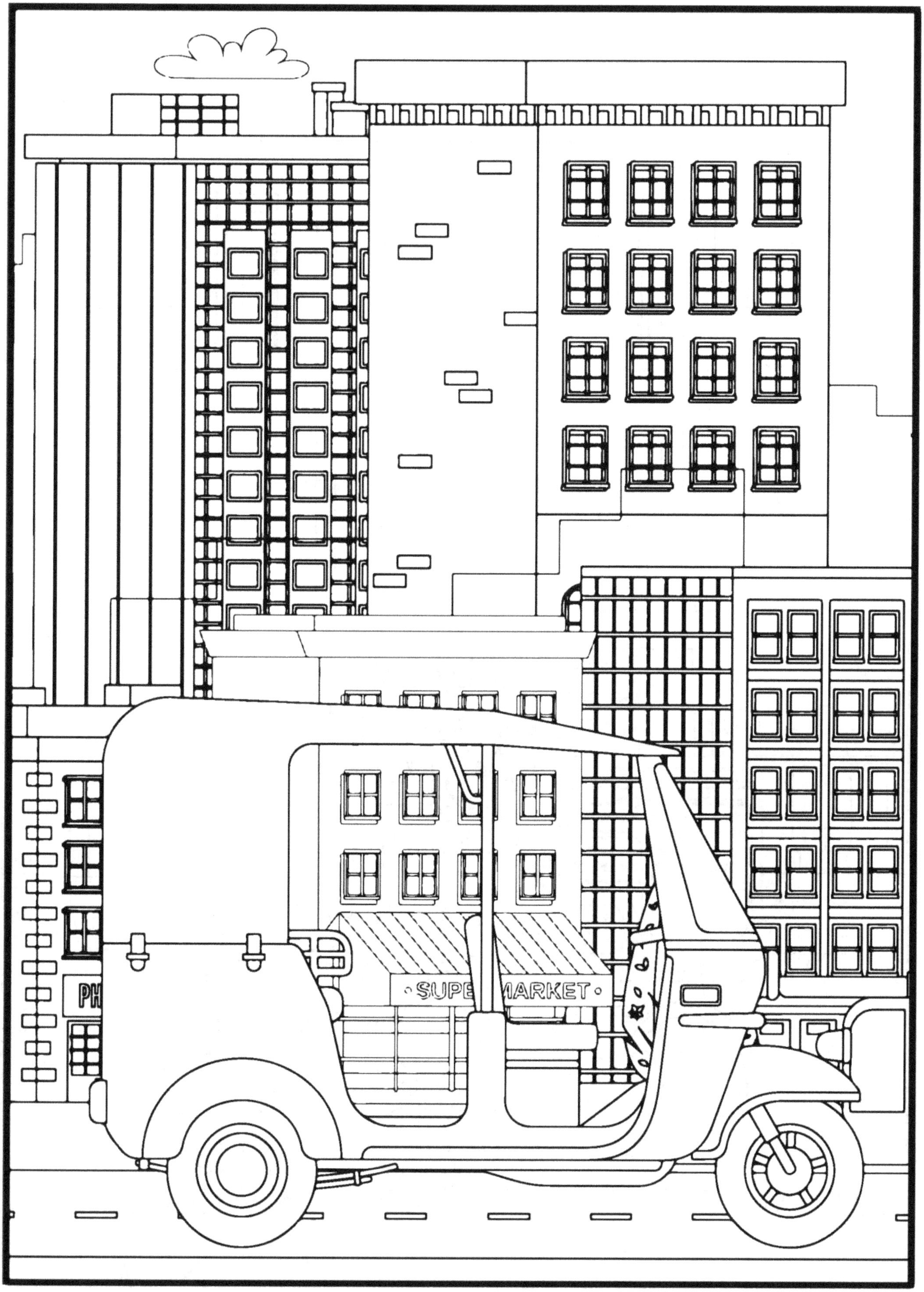
SUPE MARKET

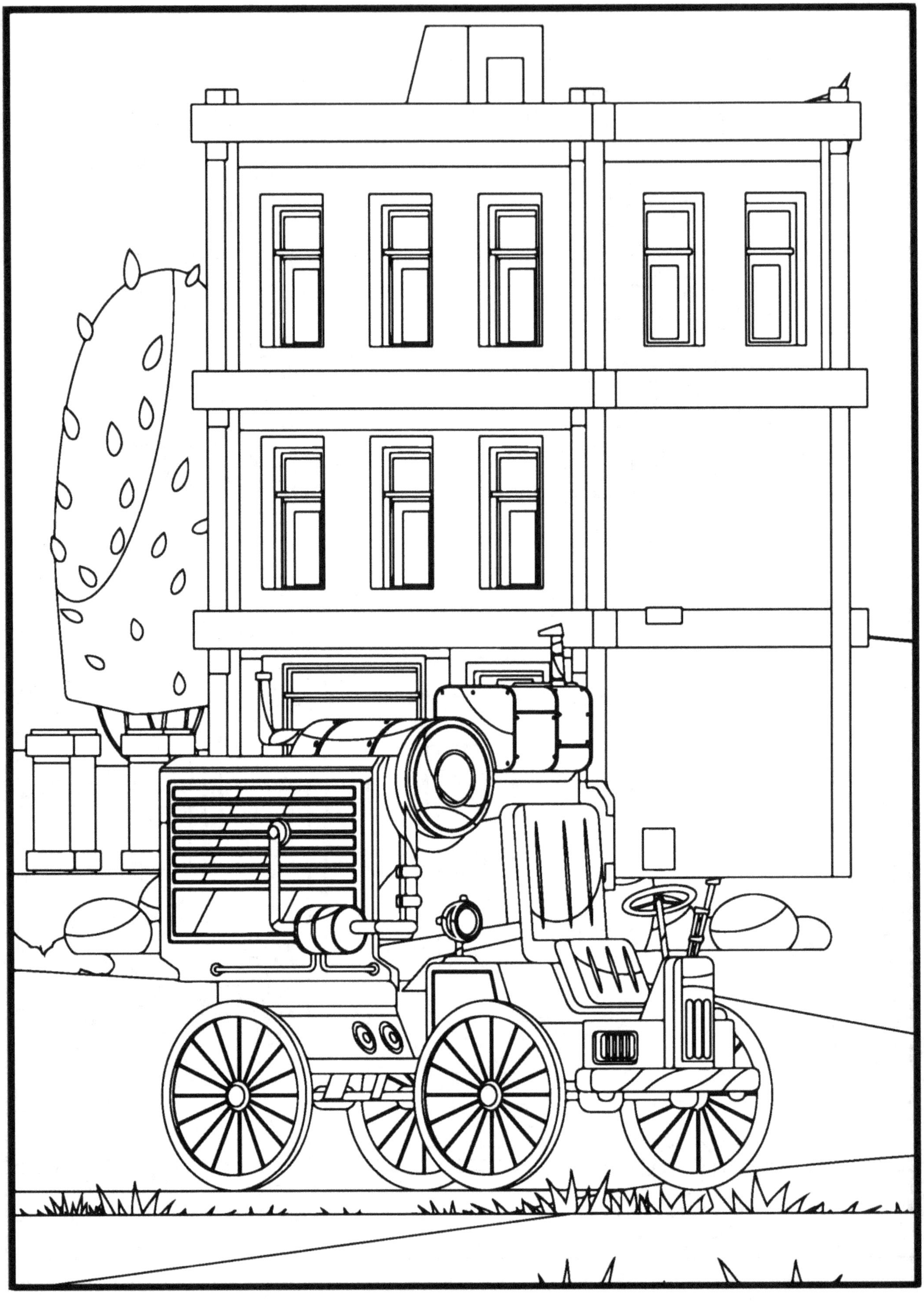

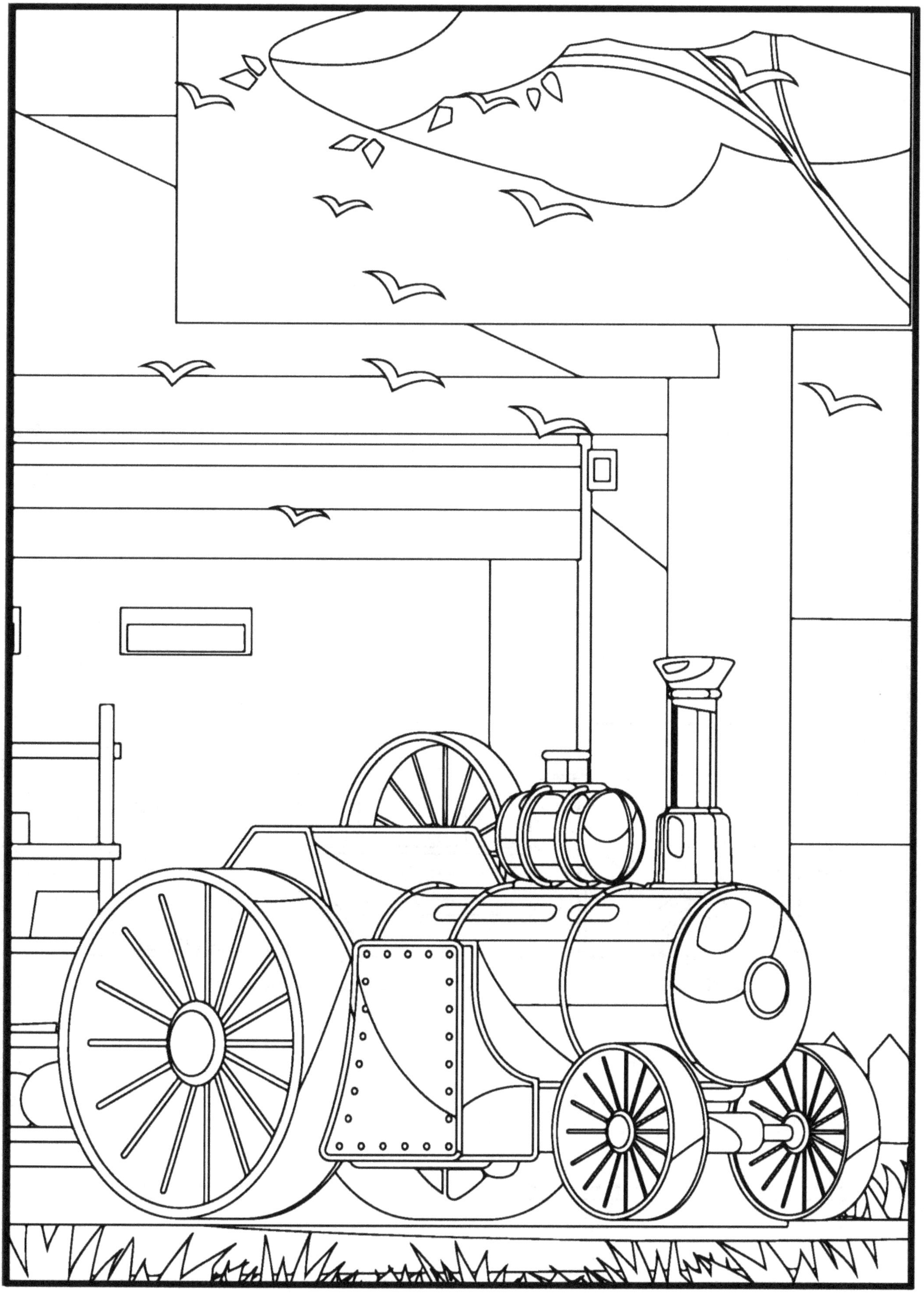

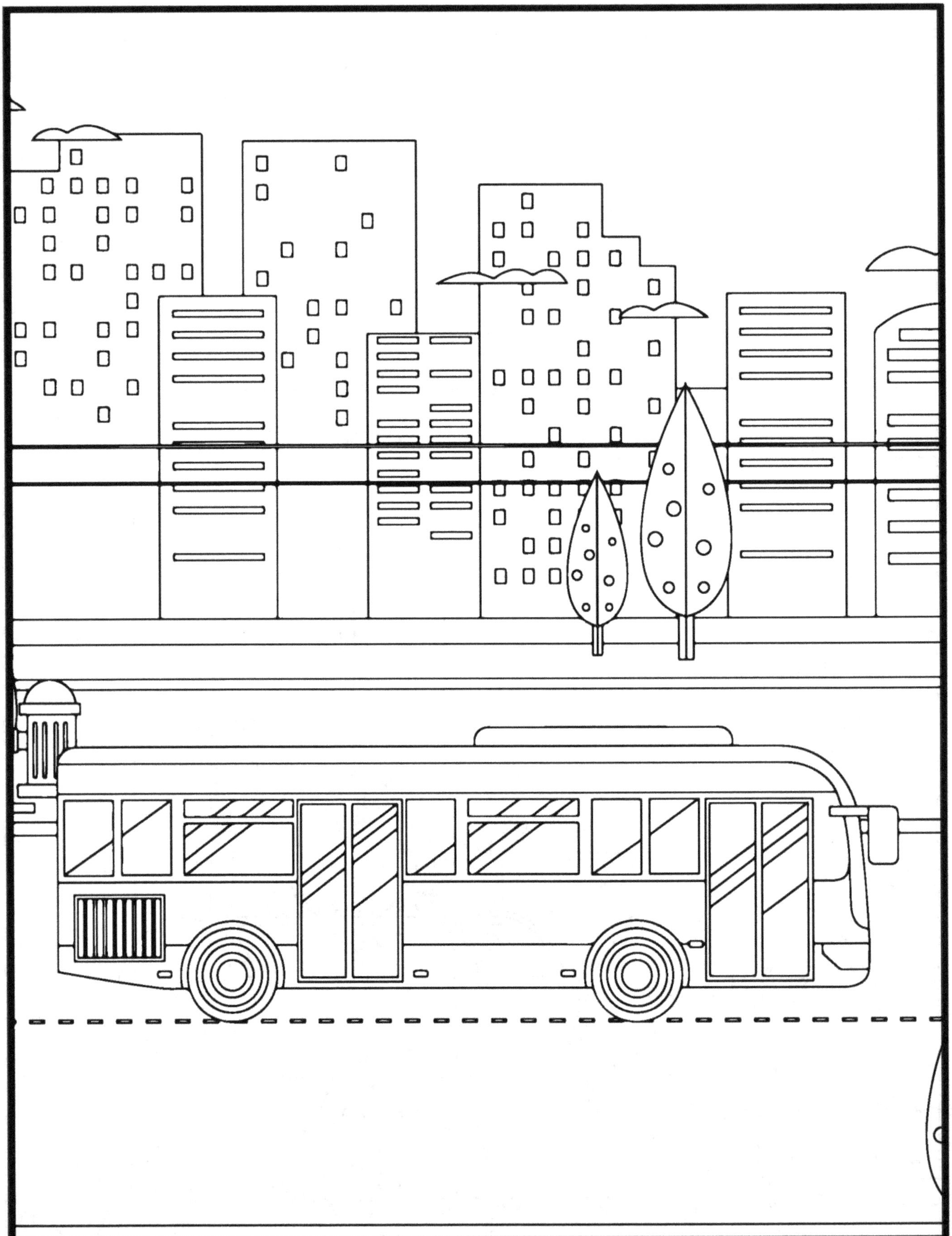

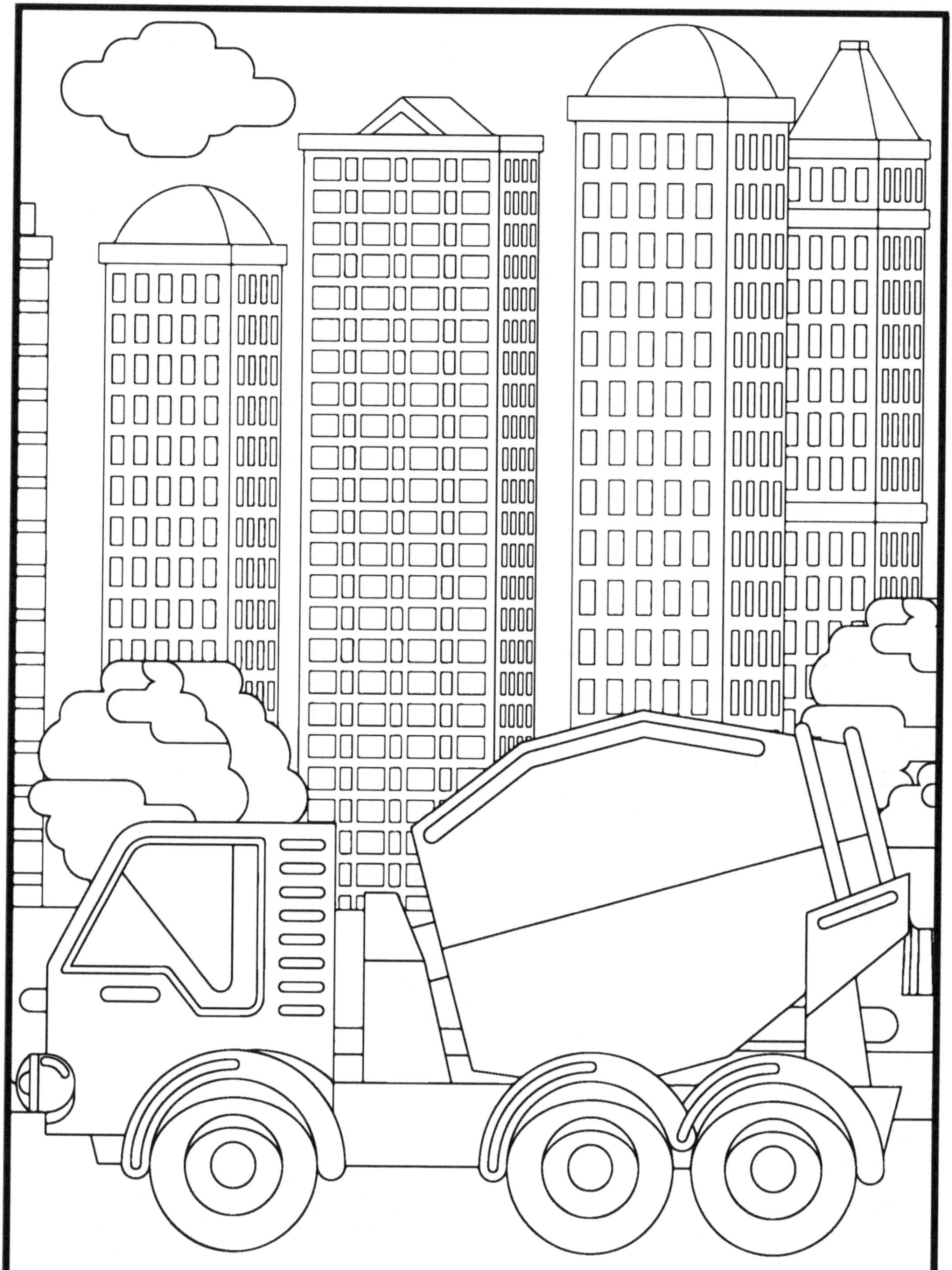

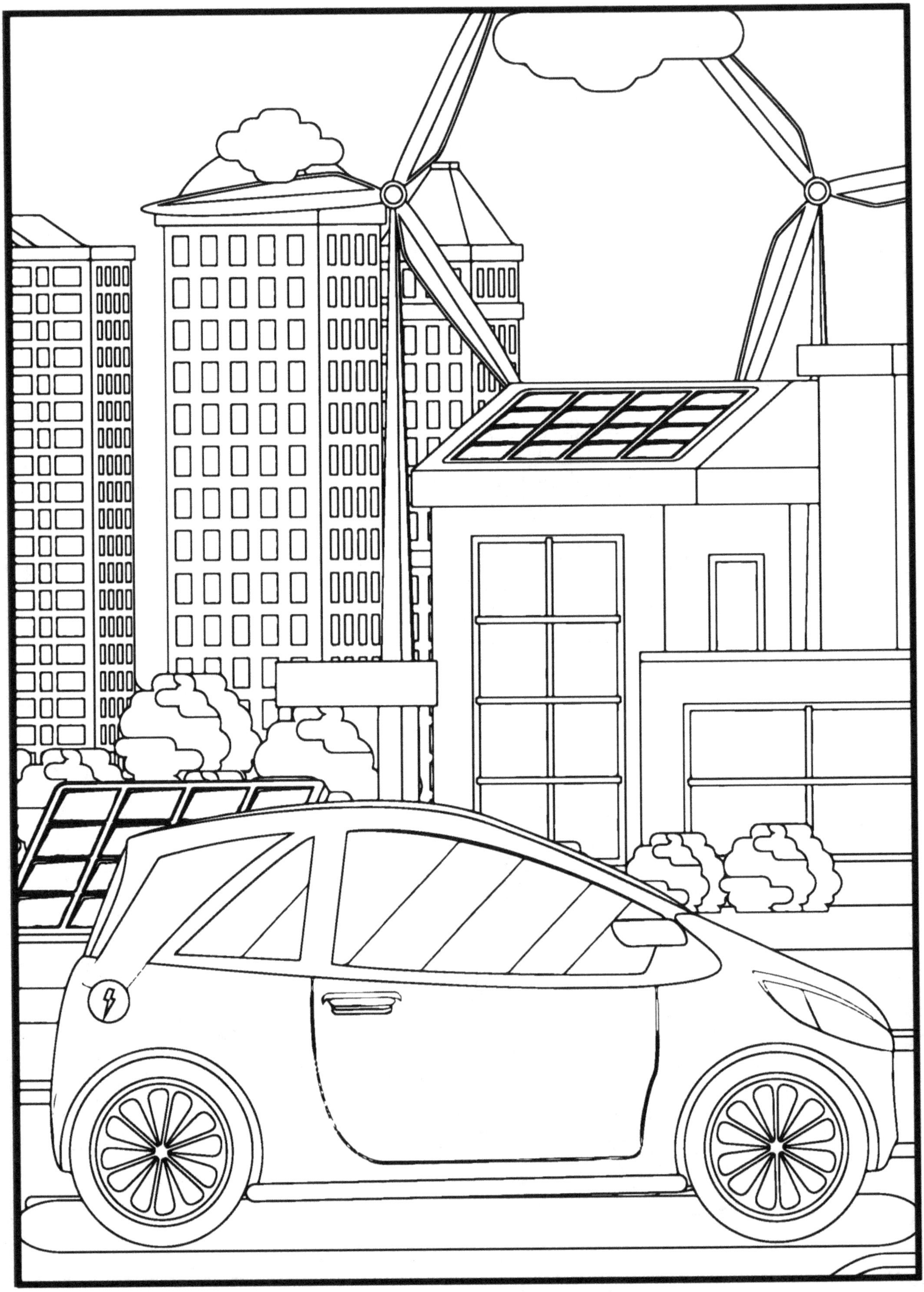

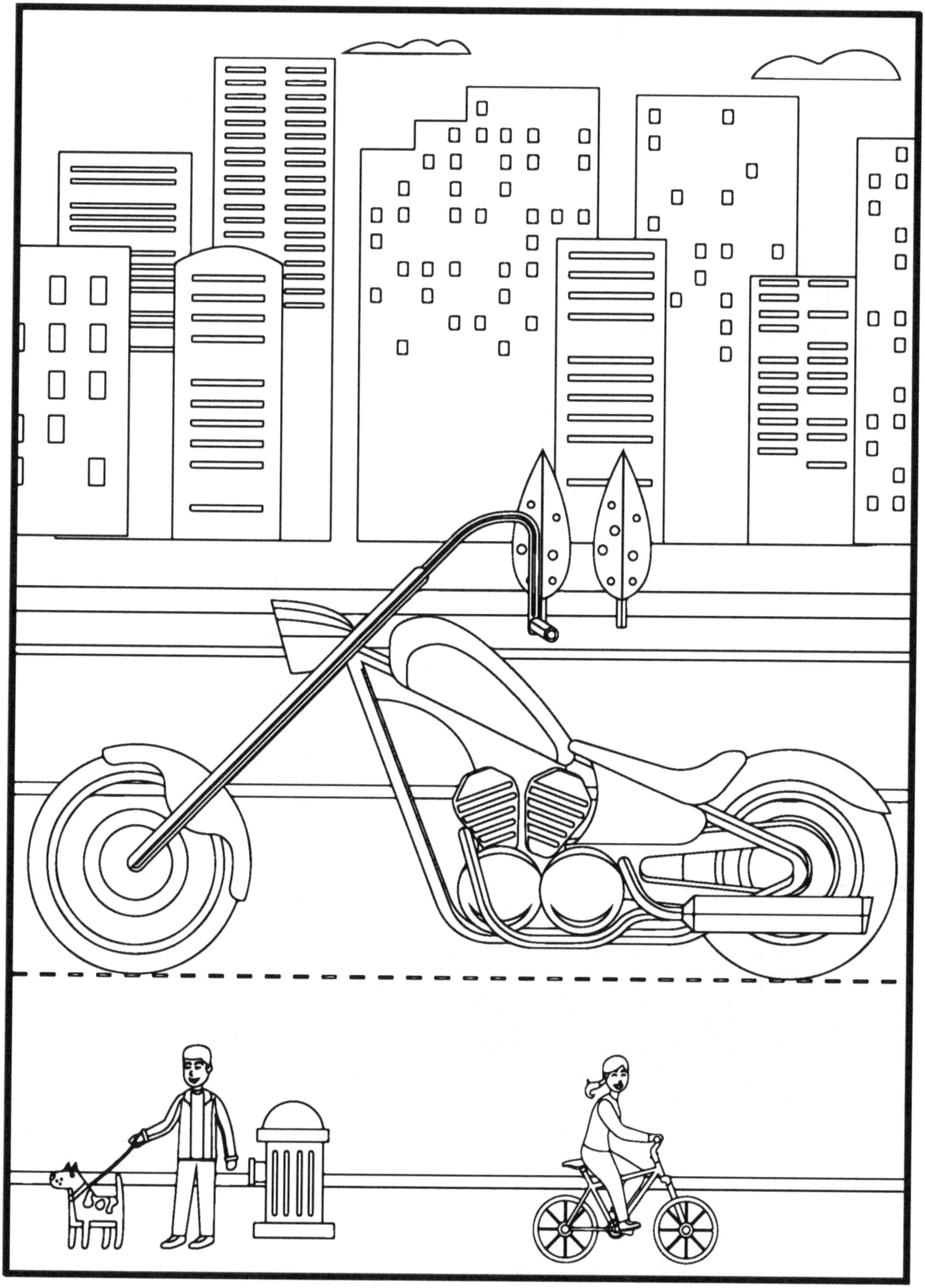

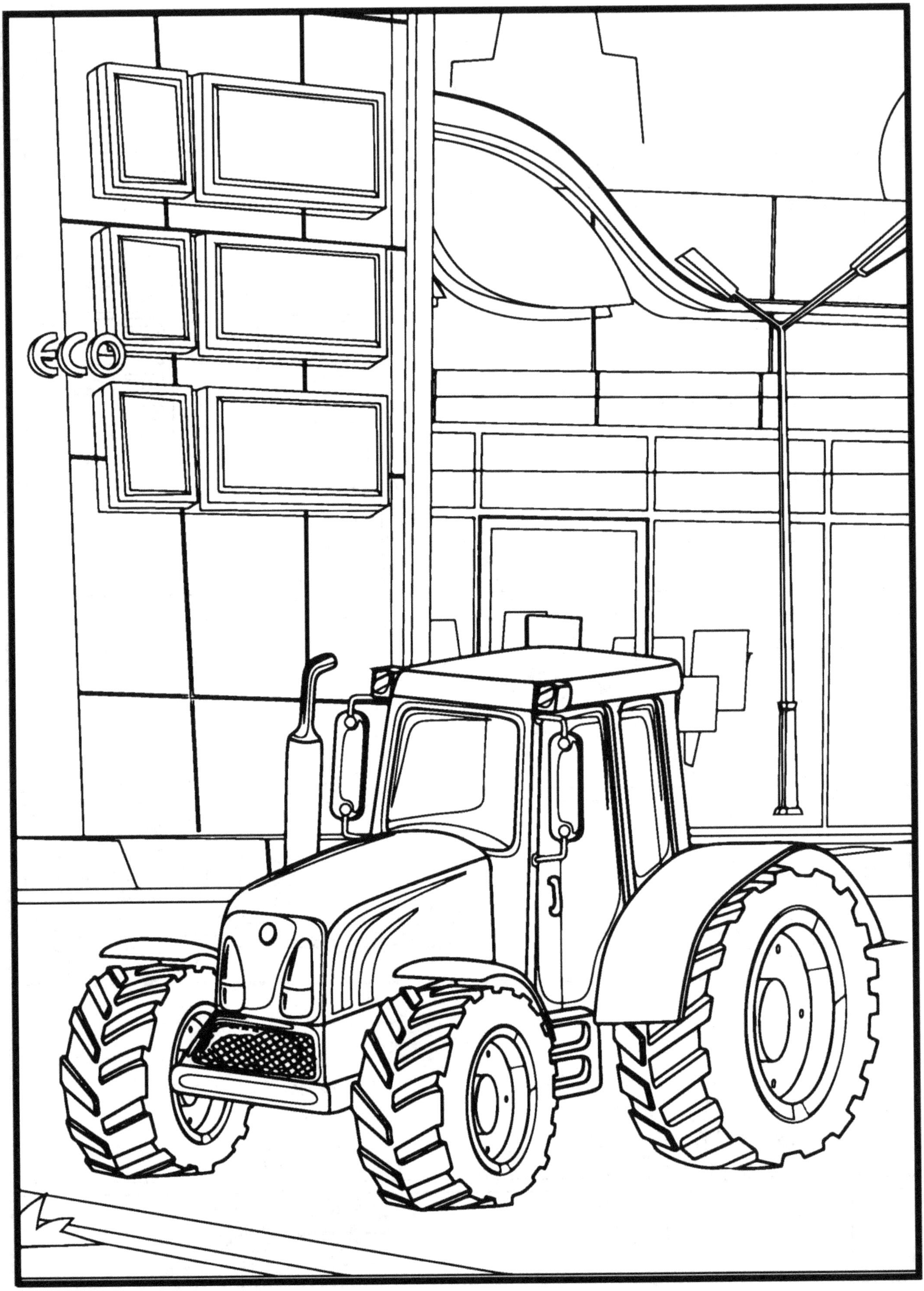
ECO

CPSIA information can be obtained
at www.ICGtesting.com
Printed in the USA
BVHW011244291121
622764BV00009B/499

9 788775 77379